Seen & Heard

100 Poems by Parents & Children
Affected by Imprisonment

Edited by Lucy Baldwin & Ben Raikes

≋ WATERSIDE PRESS

Seen & Heard
100 Poems by Parents & Children Affected by Imprisonment
Edited by Lucy Baldwin & Ben Raikes

ISBN 978-1-909976-42-9 (Paperback)
ISBN 978-1-910979-73-0 (Epub ebook)
ISBN 978-1-910979-74-7 (Adobe ebook)

Cover design © 2019 Waterside Press by www.gibgob.com

Printed in Poland by Bookpress.eu

Main UK distributor Gardners Books, 1 Whittle Drive, Eastbourne, East Sussex, BN23 6QH. Tel: +44 (0)1323 521777; sales@gardners.com; www.gardners.com

North American distribution Ingram Book Company, One Ingram Blvd, La Vergne, TN 37086, USA. Tel: (+1) 615 793 5000; inquiry@ingramcontent.com

Cataloguing-In-Publication Data A catalogue record for this book can be obtained from the British Library.

Ebook *Seen & Heard* is available as an ebook and also to subscribers of Ebrary, Ebsco, Myilibrary and Dawsonera.

Published by
Waterside Press Ltd.
Sherfield Gables, Sherfield on Loddon,
Hook, Hampshire, RG27 0JG.

Online catalogue WatersidePress.co.uk

Table of Contents

About the editors

Lucy Baldwin is Senior Lecturer in Criminology at De Montfort University Leicester. She is also a qualified Social Worker and Probation Officer having practised in her native North East. She convened the Women Family Crime and Justice Research Network at De Montfort and is the author of *Mothering Justice: Working with Mothers in Criminal Justice Settings* (Waterside Press, 2015). She specialises in research surrounding mothering in and after prison and families affected by imprisonment.

Ben Raikes is a Senior Lecturer in Social Work at Huddersfield University. He also works at the Centre for Applied Childhood, Youth and Family Research. Ben has experience as a social worker and probation officer. He runs writing groups in prisons and is a co-founder of the International Coalition for Children with Incarcerated Parents (INCCIP).

The author of the Foreword

Diane Curry OBE is the CEO of charity Partners of Prisoners and Families Support Group (POPS). She has vast experience of working within the voluntary sector and criminal justice system and is a qualified social worker. Diane received her OBE in 2006 for her pioneering work in this field including setting-up what became the Coalition for Racial Justice.

Libbie, aged 13.

Acknowledgements

First and foremost we would like to thank Lady Edwina Grosvenor for sponsoring us and then Waterside Press for turning this beautiful collection into a reality in print and virtual editions. Next and so very importantly our poetry contributors. They came from all over the UK (from many of our prisons, male and female), from Canada, Uganda, Washington and Ireland. We read, appreciated and are grateful for every single entry even though not all could be accommodated in these pages. We would especially like to thank those who facilitated the collection of our poems and worked with us the encourage contributors to send in their entries. In no particular order they are;

Sarah Burrows, Founder and Director of Children Heard and Seen (CHAS)
The CHAS team, namely Maria, James and Rod and of course the children and families
Dr Sinead O'Malley and the Mothers Project, Ireland (poems marked with an asterix)[1]
Beverley Gilbert and CoHort 4
Dr Lorna Brooks from My Time
Charlotte Parsons of PACT at HMP Eastwood Park
Michaela Booth, Patient Engagement Lead (Health in Justice), Care UK Health Care
Vanessa Garrity and New Hall and Askham Grange Prisons and Mother and Baby Unit
Wells of Hope, Uganda
HMP Parc, Wales
USA Department of Corrections, Strength in Families program
California State Prison
Sandy Watson and Victoria Elsmore at HMP Oakwood

---

1. For information about the Mothers Project and access to her thesis please contact sinead.m.omalley@gmail.com

Anawim Women's Centre, Birmingham
Inside Time prison newspaper, editorial and poetry team especially
Dave Roberts
Hannah Shead and the team at Trevi House
Ashleigh House, Coolmine, Ireland
Sofia Buncy at Muslim Women in Prison
Kirsten Godfrey Restorative Justice project in San Francisco

It is not possible to list and give credit to every single individual who supported us including by repeating and re-tweeting our calls for submissions, but please know that without your help, and that of everyone already listed above, this book would not have been possible. We are grateful to and thank you all.

Last but most certainly not least, we would like to thank Bryan and Alex Gibson, for their endless patience, their willingness to take a chance on this book and their belief in our project.

Lucy & Ben
April 2019

This book is dedicated to the memory of all those who have lost their lives in prison and the children they left behind.

Luke, aged 12.

Foreword by Diane Curry OBE

I was delighted to be asked to write this foreword for this important book, important because it gives voice to those who often go unheard. Voices that are muffled or disguised in academic papers, policy documents or reports—whereas this book provides a rare opportunity for voices to he heard in their purest form, untampered, raw and powerful. Like those of parents or children like Jordan.

Jordan is eleven and is getting up for school today. It feels normal enough, his mum appears a bit more agitated than usual and Nana and his mum's friend Jean are already at the house, which is a bit unusual, but he thinks nothing of it. He gets himself ready, kisses mum goodbye and sets off to school. On his way to school he thinks back to how mum held him for a while longer than she would usually, something wasn't quite right, but he shrugs it off and continues on his journey.

When he returns, Nana and Jean are still in the house and that feeling of something being 'not quite right' comes over him again. Nana looks like she has been crying and he asks where mum is. Nana starts crying again and Jean tries to comfort him but all he wants to know is where mum is. He doesn't hear the details, the words are not making any sense. But what he does hear is that mum has been to court and has been sent to prison.

Nobody knows where she will end up, when he will hear from her and for how long she will be away. His whole world has just been turned upside down. The sense of loss is acute, the feeling of anxiety, not only for himself but for his mum, is immense, and right here, right now, his life has changed forever.

This situation is experienced daily by children across the country (and other countries). We still don't know the actual number of children who face this situation in the UK but the Ministry of Justice estimates it to be circa 200,000. In 2013 this figure was twice the number of children affected by divorce and two-and-a-half times the number of children in 'care'.

Currently there is no routine identification or data collection process by local authorities, prisons, police departments or children's services concerning children affected by parental imprisonment and there is no statutory requirement to ensure staff working in these sectors understand the impact of imprisonment on the families they provide services to. In essence, these children are not identified, not acknowledged, not supported and not prioritised.

Research has shown that the impact of parental imprisonment has a negative effect on children's wellbeing, their increased risk of developing mental health issues, for their behaviour at home and in school to decline, and the potential for additional psychological trauma to manifest, if not identified and supported.[1]

Children's voices often go unnoticed, unheard and are mainly misunderstood. Adults tend to put their own interpretation on what they say, often missing the vital signs which also identify what is not being said. They are deeply affected when a parent is imprisoned yet they are overlooked at every stage of the criminal justice process and we miss an opportunity to reduce their trauma, understand their feelings and to provide them with the support they themselves identify they need.

Imprisoned parents often describe how the label of 'prisoner' can subsume their parental identity; the poems of the parents in this book show clearly that they are mothers and fathers before they are prisoners. Both children and parents have been given a voice in this book, providing powerful, emotive descriptions of their experiences.

The book, a collection of poems written by children and parents affected by imprisonment who are feeling the loss of a loved one, the pain of separation, goes some way to ensure that children whose plight is like Jordan's are able to share their feelings relating to the imprisonment of a parent or other loved one.

If the aim of it is to give voice to those who have an experience to share then it will require more than the reader to glance over the written contributions, it will mean digesting and then acting upon the stories they share, in their own words, or their voice will remain unheard. It is

---

1. COPING: *Children of Prisoners: Interventions and Mitigations to Strengthen Mental Health 2010-2013.*

both a testimony to each contributor's resilience and a call for action to seek positive change.

As the CEO of an organization that supports families in their endeavours to cope with the imprisonment of loved ones, I have witnessed the acceptance, the anger, the frustrations and also the resilience of families first hand. I have drawn upon my own experience of supporting a loved one through a similar process. Indeed, POPS was founded on the recognition of the value of harnessing the collective voice of those who often go unnoticed, who feel that they have no control over the circumstances they find themselves in and who live with the stigma of enforced separation and loss on a daily basis.

I am pleased to say that many years ago POPS' voice was heard and that there have been improvements to the physical conditions we endure as we visit the prisons where our loved ones are held. However, the voices of our young people, our children and their extended families still inform me that there is a long way to go before the imprisonment of a loved one has minimal negative impact on those who have committed no crime.

I am asking those of you who take time to read this book to consider what you can do to help, not only in any personal situation you may be able to relate to, but in your professional capacity, to include the voices of children and families in the design and delivery of your support services.

In Jordan's situation he has a loving family to help him to come to terms with his loss but they will also need the wider community to accept its responsibility to assist and this book will go some way to be part of that process.

I am grateful to both Lucy Baldwin and Ben Raikes for giving me the opportunity to play a small part in the culmination of this wonderful book. Having such strong allies ensures that we continue to raise awareness of the issues and, with that, have a real chance to reduce the stigma and ensure children like Jordan become visible to all who should see them.

'Never doubt that a small group of thoughtful, committed citizens can change the world, indeed it's the only thing that ever has'.

Margaret Mead, Cultural Anthropologist.

Original cover artwork by Matilda Brookes-Jones, aged ten.

Introduction

This book came about primarily because of a woman, in a prison I (Lucy) met during my work in prison. As I was leaving, the mother thrust her heart-rending poem 'Drifting Away' into my hand and said to me,

'Please read this, for me and my child, please read this and show someone in government who makes the decisions that mean we get sent here, make them see the harm it causes'.

Drifting Away

I was taken without warning, no time to prepare me, to prepare you
Wrenched screaming from court, you not knowing, blissfully unaware
You're staying with friends, taken in, in pity, the outsider
We connect after days of mutual torture, fast words, anger, recrimination, loss
Pain
You hate me, I love you, a few short months, I'm sorry, driven by desperation
Every day, I heard your pain, you were adrift, untethered, a boat with no anchor
Drifting further away
The day came and went, no call, no you, where were you, the late-night knock on my door?
You were 'missing', they didn't want to worry me, they found you
In the woods, you left a note, it was too much, you are sorry, you felt lost
You drifted away
I'm still here, now I'm lost, I'm drifting too, I never want to leave
I don't want to be in the world outside, not without you
But I will. I owe you...to live my life and yours—and to live it well
No more drifting, but anchors, a mooring, a safe crossing
In your honour.

Danielle, a mum in prison at the time of writing.

Ben leads a writing project with women in New Hall Prison and was already very aware of the power of prose and poetry, so together we decided that this book would provide not only an outlet for mothers', fathers' and children's voices, but also a 'body of evidence', straight from the horses mouth if you will, that reveals the often hidden impact of parental imprisonment.

The poems in this collection reflect the thoughts, feelings and experiences of mums and dads in and after prison and the voices of their children. Some of the 'children' are writing as grown-ups looking back over an experience they have not forgotten, often one that has profoundly affected them. Others are writing with a parent currently in prison, our youngest child poet was aged five — our oldest 'child' is in their 30s.

Our mum and dad poets write about their hopes and fears, their pain at being separated from their children. Some may not have had custody of their children prior to prison, some may not on release, yet they remain parents, traumatised by the effect their life choices and life chances have had on their children. They write about some of the pain and trauma that led them to prison, what it feels like for them inside prison, and what they hope for on release.

Some of our parents are reflecting backwards on their experience of prison as a parent and the position they found themselves in. This book is not about judgement — it is simply a space created, a platform given, to facilitate the voices of these parents and their children being heard.

Ben and I both work with people who are living in and after prison and we feel passionately that their voices — and especially the voices of their children, are so often muted, missing or silenced. Subsumed in facts and figures and scandalous headlines. We wanted to remind readers that behind every statistic is a human being, a story, a life; somewhere around every parent who is sent to prison is a child — a child who serves the sentence with their parent, albeit most often outside, and in a different way, but they serve the sentence, nonetheless.

Children are sometimes permanently separated from their parent as a result of his or her sentence, but whether the separation is permanent or temporary there is no doubt it is painful, confusing and challenging.

Wherever the children are from, or whatever country parents are incarcerated in, these feelings are universal.

Some of the poems are happy poems, looking only forwards with optimism and excitement; some are sad, tragic poems that reveal the profound hurt of parental imprisonment; others, most in fact, are a mix of the two—reflecting the complexity of human emotion in relation to this form of separation. All bear witness to lives interrupted, dreams dashed or postponed, but the true message of the book is hope.

Hope for a future where fewer are incarcerated, thus meaning fewer parents and their children experience the often unnecessary separation by miles and bars; further hope that it will inspire readers to activism in relation to doing something, however small, a donation, volunteering, a shift in attitude, a kind thought—something that honours the willingness of the poets in these pages to share their thoughts and emotions.

We than you for your purchase. Royalties from the book will be donated to two separate bodies supporting children of imprisoned parents, namely the charity Children Heard and Seen (childrenheardandseen. co.uk) and the organization My Time (www.mytimeltd.org.uk). The charity and organization do wonderful work and are led, respectively, by Sarah Burrows and Lorna Brooks, two amazing selfless, determined women who give of their best every day, to make a difference to the lives of children affected by imprisonment. Neither organization is currently permanently funded and both rely completely on goodwill and donations to survive. We sincerely hope this will change in the future, and that Government will recognise the need for children of imprisoned parents to be appropriately and fully supported—and that they are able to demonstrate this via permanent funding.

A recent report highlighted that parental imprisonment affects 100,000 more children than previously thought, 295,000 by paternal imprisonment alone.[2] We know that children with a parent in prison are more likely to be negatively affected emotionally, financially, educationally and socially. We also know they are more likely to become offenders. As

---

2. Kincaid, Roberts and Kane (2019), 'Children of Prisoners: Fixing a Broken System', Crest, University of Nottingham. Available at www.nicco.org.uk/directory-of-resources/children-of-prisoners-a-report-from-crest-advisory

there is no formal collection of data about children affected by parental imprisonment, not even correct statistics, we are currently missing golden opportunities in terms of welfare, intergenerational crime prevention — and most importantly — support for children and families affected by it. This must change. The voices in this book are powerful testimony to the reasons why.

CHAPTER 1

Poems Written by Mums In or After Prison

In the UK alone it is estimated that 312,000 children are affected by imprisonment annually,[1] 17,000 of these will be children separated from their mothers. Most often for sentences of less than six months, but also for much shorter periods, measured in weeks rather than months. Despite the brevity of the sentence, when a mother is imprisoned the consequences can be devastating. Only five per cent of children remain in their own home, many are displaced to be cared for by local authorities, multiple relatives, fathers and friends.[2] Siblings are often separated and visits to see their mums are not always possible[3]—due to distance from prisons and cost implications. The situation for mums and children, especially in the UK is significantly more challenging than for men in prison because of the location of women's prisons. Many children remain between 60–150 miles away from their mothers, making visits sometimes impossible.

Mothers in and after prison speak about just how important it is to them that they can maintain links with family, especially children. Mothers in prison will often say 'I'm a mother first', it remains important to be as involved in their children's lives as possible, to be able to mother from prison and to prepare for release.[4] For those mothers who do not have care of their children and who may not resume care on release, it remains vital that their maternal emotions are supported and acknowledged, it can quite simply be a matter of life or death.[5]

1. Kincaid, Roberts and Kane (2019) 'Children of Prisoners: Fixing a Broken System', Crest, University of Nottingham available at www.nicco.org.uk/directory-of-resources/children-of-prisoners-a-report-from-crest-advisory
2. Caddle D and Crisp, D (1997), *Imprisoned Women and Mothers*, London: Home Office.
3. Baldwin and Epstein (2017), 'Short But Not Sweet: A Study Exploring the Impact of Short Custodial Sentences on Mothers and their Children', Oakdale Trust, Montfort University. Available at www.nicco.org.uk/directory-of-resources/lucy-baldwin-works-on-maternal-imprisonment
4. Baldwin L (2018), 'Motherhood Disrupted: Reflections of Post-prison Mothers', *Emotion Space and Society*, 26: 49-56 https://doi.org/10.1016/j.emospa.2017.02.002
5. Baldwin, L (Ed) (2015), *Mothering Justice: Working with Mothers in Criminal and Social Justice Settings*, Hook: Waterside Press.

The Moon the Stars and the Sun

You are not just my child, my genes.
You are my strength my armour my dreams.
Without you life would be so dark, and I could not find any hope or spark.
Without you this world would just feel so cold.
You made my destiny beautiful, it's not just to grow old.
I cherish every second you grace this world.
You are my idols, I am so proud.
Your eyes made from diamonds, your smile the stars.
Life can never separate us no distance is too far.
One day I will be free, to be the mummy I always wanted to be.
I know you already know, I know you do.
All that has ever come easy to me, is not living but being a mummy.
I'm lost without you.
So sleep tight and look to the moon tonight,
It knows I am always there, you can still feel the warmth of my care.
So be strong and look after each other.
Because I am your mummy not just another mother.

Jade, a mum in prison.

Perfect Mum

Shame, regret, sadness and guilt,
Devastation and breakdown of relationships built,
Prison, incarceration, locked up and jail,
Not the words used in a traditional mother's tale.

Separated years before — because of violence from a man,
Now living safely with my brother and his wife my least big fan.
I agreed with everything so desperate to keep ties,
Periods of long separation — no one to hear my cries.

Those children of mine are of an age,
Of knowledge, understanding of how to earn an honest wage
From a world so far away from crime
I tried so hard to hide the activities in my life time.

In the beginning I would lie, strongly deny the stories — claiming their lies
My name in the newspaper — others making those family ties
Already an absent mum in the day to day care
Playground mothers look concerned but cannot hide that stare.

One thing I questioned myself about — when others said I was mad,
Was being open and honest about my life choices good or bad,
I wanted to ensure there was nothing others could say,
They didn't already know about in some way.

Having to admit to my crimes to my child,
Looking into those eyes so meek and mild
Heartfelt shame and admitting the truth
Their acceptance — the tug of love I feel inside goes thru the roof.

My children voiced their fears of tales of violence and bullying they'd heard,
AFTER ALL I HAVE BEEN THRU 2 — don't be absurd!

Your mum aint going to take no shit,
No name calling, nastiness never bullied never hit.

From within my cell behind the wall,
I preferred to write letters instead of call,
So worried about causing distress and upset
Or for my adult son to call me 'wet'!

So much more I can put in print, so much more I can say,
More open and loving words written stronger than before I went away
Words that dance across the page,
Send a love to last an age,

When my daughter asked to visit me they're
—unsure if this is right, do I dare?
What she craved was a reassurance of such
To see for herself I okay—to tell me she loves me so very much,

A bittersweet visit I will never forget,
Excitement to see my baby that day I met,
Cuddles,

Although certainly my actions the children they not proud,
But they still fight my corner they do so loud!
As my son and daughter so often repeat,
Every card opened or the label on a treat.

You may not be the perfect MUM
But you are MY MUM,
I may not like what you do
But I LOVE every bit of you.

Nicola, a post-prison mum.

That Dreaded Night

The night I was arrested you bounced up and down on my knee,
With my fingers tickling your belly, you laughed in glee.

That wonderful moment was brought abruptly to a halt,
And I know I can't blame anyone because it's all my fault.

They knew you were there, but they broke down the door,
Snatching you from my arms and throwing me on the floor.

I was helpless when you cried and screamed in fear,
They ransacked the house and did nothing but shout and sneer.

Intisar, a post-prison mum.

Eliza, when aged 8.

Mother Inside

No matter how much I love you and wanted to stay,
That night you were forced to watch me get taken away.

You pleaded and cried when they put the handcuffs on me,
Yet they looked at me as a number and smiled in glee.

I have to do the sentence and it's all my mistake,
But how much are they going to punish me for God's sake?!

At the end of the tunnel I can't seem to see the light,
In this place the days are mixed with the night.

The day before I was arrested, we shopped for your pram,
By the time I get out of prison, you will have forgotten who I am.

My heart yearns to hold you close and keep you near,
But this is not a place for a two-month-old my dear.

Amal, a post-prison mum.

Luke, aged 13.

Prison bars

She gives the prison bars a shake,
And she screams until her belly aches
'Why me!' she cries in the cold box,
Is time going backwards on the clock?
Finally, she goes back home,
Sees her Eliza and Yassin at the door,
Mum, are you okay? Yes,
'Are you sure?'
I feel so dumb,
I regret what I did,
I acted like a little kid,
Please forgive me and forget the past,
Don't worry mum,
The time has passed,
I just wanted to let you know,
I love you so much,
Both of you are my heros!
Love u loads mummy they say.

Natacha, a post-prison mum.

Thoughts and Feelings

Having to leave my children without a choice
Left me with feelings near on impossible to voice
But I'm going to try so that you
Have some insight on what we go through

At first there's this unforgettable feeling
A feeling I've told many feels like grieving
My heart was torn apart what will I do
With this hurt of being so far away from you
When will I see them what will they know?
Where am I going to say mummy had to go?
Do I be truthful, or do I lie
All I want now is to curl up and die

Who will cuddle them and tuck them in bed?
So many questions go round in your head
What are they doing now are they happy?
Who's going to change my baby's nappy
Do they get up on time are their school clothes clean?
What if their friends find out and start being mean?
The pain and guilt riddle me inside
Lost count of all the times I've cried
Feeling like I need to be saved
From this want for you the biggest thing I've craved

Another night and the questions start
Tearing shreds out of my broken heart
Are they okay are they playing?
Who and what have people been saying?
What cartoons are they watching what do they like?
Who's going to teach them how to ride their bike's
The list goes on as you lay awake at night
I'm lucky I've got the chance to put things right

Only twice in five months I've got to hold you
I know it's not much but the best I could do
Only a couple more months and we can make this more often
The rest of my life ill make up for you feeling forgotten
For now, one day at a time we've got to get through
But mummy's coming back. remember... mummy loves you.

Karen, a post-prison post rehab mum.

Always There

I wish I could go back to the day I held you tight
When you was close to me and I kissed you goodnight
The days when I was close as the rain
Not lost in all that is wrong, all this pain driving me insane
It should be me who wipes your tears, chases your fears
Gives you tea
Be there for you from morning to night
Your memory should not be something I have to fight
Why do I feel you fading into the past?
When we are destiny and we should last
Every teardrop, every smile with you
By my side they seemed worthwhile
All the words we have left unspoken
Seep into the cracks that in my heart are broken
I feel cold
My body, my heart feel old
Just know I'm here so you can shine
Be bright, illuminate your light
I will stand strong if you ever need fight
Wherever you go whatever you do
No power of man can stop me loving you
So just know I am there
There is never a moment I don't care
Every second of every day
I promise I will always find a way
To give you strength to face the day
Chase the monsters, make them go away
My beautiful child do not cry
Nothing will make me give up or say goodbye.

Jade, a mum in prison.

My Children

Have you ever left your children?
Have you ever felt the pain?
Have you ever felt those teardrops?
That fell like falling rain
If you never left your children
I pray you never do
Coz the day I left my children
My heart was broke in two

I'm in the Dochas for my crime
My kids also doing the time
Although they visit every week
The time we share I'll always keep
I'm suffering now for my past
But my love for them will always last
No matter what they're always there
And that's because I'll always care
If you've never left your children
I pray you never do.

*Grace a prison mum.**

Pride and Joy

My pride, my joy, I love you so much
It's hard being away, the only thing that keeps me going
Is knowing you're okay
To see your face, to watch you smile
I never stop thinking of you, always on my mind

You always make me laugh, you never make me cry
The only thing that makes me sad
Is not seeing you all the time
These thick brick walls, these steady bars
Being locked behind them is so very hard

Waiting for the day, we can be together
I promise you my little one
Our lives are gonna get better
Mammy made mistakes, she wishes she could change
All that gets me through the night
Is you my little star
Knowing that you are safe outside
Knowing where you are

I know I've made mistakes
I wish I could take them back
I promise darling when I get out
I'll always have your back

I know you need your mammy
Your mammy needs you too
I promise you my little one
I'll do whatever I have to do

You're my world, my universe
The one that makes me smile
You and me together again
I'm yours and you are mine
My little angel
You've been through so much
You're so full of life
Your hugs your kisses
Your beautiful smile
Your fingers and toes
You make me so happy
It fills me inside
So full of passion and of hope.

*Lyndsey, a mum in prison.**

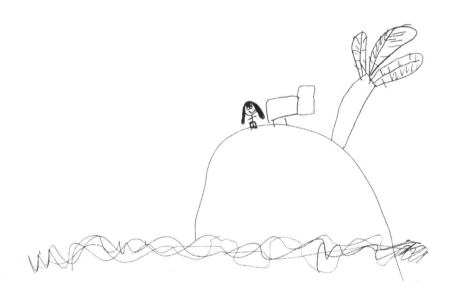

Sarah, aged seven, with a parent in prison.

God's Good Grace

Three hundred inmates, but I'm so alone
I don't need more people, I just wanna go home!
I eagerly consume all the hours and days
Using my time in a myriad of ways
Until you've been here you haven't a clue
But then who am I to cast judgement on you?

Murderers smackheads, drug-dealers or slags
Forgive the ignorant for their obsession with tags
'We' have been called many times in our lives
Mothers of children, lovers and wives
'We've' done many things, and that's what's so sad
They forget all the good, just remember the bad

I know I'm no saint, but I'm more than my crime
And I hope for forgiveness in the fullness of time
I'm never alone when regrets crowd my mind
With the thoughts of the damage that I left behind
So, before you cast judgement, put yourself in my place
For I could easily be you, but for god's good grace!

*Sarah, a post-prison mum.**

Without a Trace

When I wish upon a star
I always wonder where you are
Are you near or are you far?
I just want to know where you are

I look into the distance
And slowly see you fade
Just to see your face one more time
For this both arms I would trade

When I try to remember you
I cannot see your face
It's like you've disappeared
Gone without a trace

I know God has his reasons
For taking you away
But I really wasn't prepared for this
I always thought you'd stay

I will never forget the memories
I hold down so deep
Nobody can ever take them away,
They'll always be mine to keep.

Rizzo, a mum not only separated from her children, but also the child of
a mum who went to prison. Her mum died whilst she was in prison.*

My Baby and Me

We are here together
In this fishbowl
They watch, they wait
Will I fall, will I fail

For you, for you I will do this
I can't fail,
I wont lose you too
I would not survive

We will do this together
You and me
Against the world
We'll show them

One day this will be a memory,
For me not for you
You and me baby
I'm doing it for you.

Laura and Laurie Lee aged four months in a prison Mother and Baby Unit.

LIFE

Life they said
A life sentence for me
But this is not life
It's not living
I'm not free

You will grow up without me
A whole life on your own
Nothing left for me to do
Ill be here, and you'll be grown

Birthdays, Christmases, school,
Loves, children, holidays. It all
No one to love you
To catch you when you fall

No brothers or sisters
Not from me anyway
Just the two of you
Alone you will play

No life here for me
But live yours. Be free
No life her for me
Live yours
Forget me.

Sandy, sentenced to life imprisonment when her twins were four-years-old.

Heart Pain

My Heart it hurts when I think of you
I did what I did
I do what I do
It's wrong and I know it
But I can't stop
One more pill
One more shop

But now I'm here
And you are gone
Because on that day
I did wrong
They took you forever
I won't see you never

I'm still your mum
I'll always be
One day I'll be clean
You watch you see
Too late for us
My tears like rain
When I think of you my heart's in pain.

Molly, a young mum in prison.

You Lot

I miss you all
The tears, the snot
The nappies, the grime
The carpet of slime
The Lego,, the bricks
The Playdoh the tricks
I miss you lot

I miss the love
The hugs
The cuddles and tugs
The play fights
The rolling on my rugs
I miss you lot

Ill be home soon
And we can do all the above
I'll kiss you, tickle you
Fill you up with love
I miss you lot
But not for long.

Mummy's home next week.

Adisa, a mum in prison.

If Only

The day my grandma was laid to rest
May 25th a day I'll never forget
I should have been there to say goodbye
Instead I was in a police cell asking myself why
A moment of madness, a stupid decision made
If only I hadn't picked up that blade
I was protecting my daughter
I told them over and over again
Little did I know
How much trouble I was in
Months on bail, not knowing my fate
Waiting on the judge to decide on the final date
Racked with guilt and full of shame
My unstable moods I was sure to blame
A guinea pig for medication the doctor said would be fine
But I was still battling this crazy mad head of mine
Thinking about what led me to this hell
A better person I'd like to be

Ill learn from this and change you'll see
My family my friends they all had to suffer
My beautiful daughter left with no mother
I have the chance to gain the qualifications I lack
I will do my time and never come back
I will get all the help I need
To show everyone that I can succeed
The days all crossed off, that's another week done
I miss my life, I miss being a mum
I think of all my mistakes and what I can learn
To make my family proud, that's what I yearn
Home is the place that I long to be
Being reunited with friends, with family
No more Drake Hall, I will finally be free
Back to my little girl
Just how it used to be.

Carly, a Mum in prison.

Eliza, Yassin and Leyah.

I Am a Mother

I love you I love you
I want to protect you
I can't in here
How can I be victimised for trying to protect you?
No one listens, no one cares
A child is not a prisoner
Must not be a prisoner
I won't be scared
I am strong
I refuse to be broken
I hope to heal from this horror
I want to feel like a mother
I am a mother.

Memory, a mother on an MBU whose child was removed from her care and made to live 'outside'.

Me and You

Me and you we are a team
Me and you we are a dream
Me and you we belong together
Me and you we are strong together
Me and you we are each other's heart
Me and you we need a fresh start
Me and you the stars and the moon
Will all be ours when mum's home soon
Me and you
Always.

Wendy, a mum in prison.

It Isn't Easy

Being in jail isn't easy
Being away from your loved ones
The people you care about
Having all these mixed-up feelings
Wanting to scream and cry and shout

I hate people knowing where I am
And I do feel the shame
But I'm the one whose doing time
And they don't feel my pain
The way I feel about myself
The person I was and want to be now
All I need is a push and shove
And someone to show me how

To not be able to hold your child
To tell them everything's alright
To not be able to put them to bed
To kiss and hold them tight.

*Extract from Poem by Lyndsey, a mum in prison.**

Ten Minutes Out of Your Day

Getting locked up is the shttiest thing ever.
you feel like you aint getting out. Ever
so I get remanded
thrown on the prison bus until we landed
all I could think about was FFS I'm rattling 'ere
what am i going to do without any gear
I go into panic mode... start to sweat
I know for a fact it was happening
this weren't no bet
soon as we arrived at reception
girls were asking
what you in for
fraud and deception
I had all these emotions and feelings
there was nothing here for a quick fix healing

the prison guards look you up and down
with a stinking frown
they've already judged you
how have I got in this situation
I haven't a clue
we are no longer members of society
we are scum
this was my life
it's the furthest from fun
the prison guards are laughing, having a smoke on the
yards
we are not called by are first name
I swear it's is like the crying game

women's prisons are so different to the men's
'cause the men have their visits boxed
and we just hoping for a visit

the guards shout our surname
undo the locks
the hardest part for me
was me and the kids being apart
when I think about it now
it still breaks my heart

Where's mummy? I want her home now
with tears in my eyes... when... how?
My mum had two of my kids
she didn't have any support
she didn't know what to do
how to book a visit
she didn't have a clue
there was no-one to give her advice or empathise
It's like 'your daughter's a smack head'
she's better off in prison
probably end up dead
I've turned my life around since then
my life has gone from zero to ten
but one thing I know for sure
this prison aint no cure
and if my mum have had one family support worker
to say hey, let me help you, I promise your gonna be okay
she needed someone to guide her
that's all she would need
so whoever reads this
please take heed
prison has a ripple effect on all loved ones
so just ask if they okay
please take ten minutes out of your day.

Diane, a mum and ex-prisoner, now working
with families affected by incarceration.

My Children

Children are amazing
Children are the best
When I'm with my children
I get butterflies in my chest.

Kelly-Anne, a mum in prison.

Looking Back

On my way to court, don't be late they said
What a date, April 28th will never be the same
The longest day of my life, knowing I'd be leaving my girls
Oh, it was so hard, I thought it was the end, for me, for us
Emotions are high, I did not anticipate this situation
Neither did I realise it was the start of a new beginning

Now eight years have passed,
I'm in my dream job my girls are all grown up
Making great decisions, becoming successful in their lives
I'm incredibly proud of my girls, I wouldn't trade them
Or this experience, it helped make us all closer than ever.

Toni's mum, who went to prison.[6]

---

6. See also Toni's poem 'Mummy's Castle' on page 107.

Prison Makes Me feel.

like shouting

like Shouling that im angry
like Slouting that im sad mad.
like slouting what im sad
like shouting let my mumy out
I dont want to live with Dad.
LET HER GO.!

Ellen, aged 11.

Consoled by Hope

Separated and Caged, consoled by hope
My tears are seeping onto this paper as I write this
Ripped out of your life and shackled with emptiness
Justice still eludes me — bleak and sombre
My heart's companions are pain, grief and despair
Blood tears deep from the heart, gather in my eyes and pour
Longing to see your beautiful seraphic rosy face
And inhaling your deep sweet scent that is my favourite perfume
From your ringlet tendrils of golden-brown silken hair
Missing your dewy brown eyes, your voice soft and sweet
With all my strength I cut this melancholy chain
I am not defeated
Buried deep I know that mother's love is a resilient thing
You are so much in the soul of me
You have kept me alive all these years
The pride and joy of my life, only you can make this heart rejoice
I haven't and will never let you depart
I keep you safe, in the tower of my heart
My darling daughter
I look forward to our years to come
Perfectly glorious, joyous and infinity times infinity awaits
Always loving you
I am forever your affectionate and devoted mummy.

Adel, a mum and long-term prisoner.

My Babies

Nicole, my girl when you were small
You reminded me of a porcelain doll
You've made me a proud and happy mum
Just look how far you've become
You're my special star up in the sky
You're my beautiful sun in the days going by
I take out all my pictures of you
And it's you my princess that gets you through
So I want you to know I love you so much
And it's a love nobody can touch you're in my head and my heart don't forget
You're the best little girl a mummy can get

Thomas my gorgeous beautiful boy
The day you were born you gave me such joy
You were like a little teddy bear
The cutest boy I've seen in my life I swear
You know I love you, I miss you too
Look after your sister like big brothers do
I promise you son we'll be soon together
Always in my heart forever and ever.

*Christina, a mum in prison.**

Prison Girl

Prison girl went to jail one day
Then her child was taken away
When she asked the reason why
They did get this reply

You're on drugs and we don't care why
You steal from shops for your supply
We took your child and you know why
We'll crush your life in the blink of an eye
They said it would only be for a week
Little did I know the weeks turned to years

They said they would help but they dragged me down
Wouldn't stop until I hit the ground
Prison girl is going through hell
Without her child, in a prison cell
It does get tough, but we did the crime
And now our kids are doing the time

There's one more thing I have to say
To all mothers in jail
We live to fight another day.

Joanne, an Irish prison mammy.*

My Only One — My Daughter

You are my love, my happiness
My life, my light, my air

Without my love, I feel unloved
Without my happiness I feel sad
Without my life I feel dead inside
Without my light I walk in the dark
Without my air I feel both breathless and suffocated

Rosie, a mum in prison.

Lost

The day we were parted, I felt so lost
A tear in my eye, I felt so cross
What have I done?
What was it worth?
Something you don't deserve?
Being away, hurts inside
This is something I cannot hide
My heart is broke, what can I do
I wish that I could cuddle you,
Tuck you in at night
In the end it will be alright
We are lost right now
But that won't last
Soon that will be in the past.

Deborah, a mum in prison.

Edward

A clear drop falls onto his cheek,
It glistens for a moment, I was crying
Crying, because Edward was so beautiful
And yet he does not stir when a tear falls,
Warm on his skin, I could not bear it
He was my son, he belonged to me,
But too short a time, now he is gone.
His eyelids made a shadowy look, bluish and bruised
His lips pale and bloodless
As I pushed the stray hairs from his face
I could not help but notice
Just how beautiful he really was.
I closed my eyes. The pain too much
. Edward was everything to me
I sat beside him for a while
Rocking slowly back and forth
Trying to understand what just happened
But now there were things I needed to do for him
And for myself
My family said rituals help us through the difficult times
That the mourning and the burial helps
To accept both death and the need to carry on
I believe this now
I can still hear the hymns
The smell of the incense
The mumbling of the congregation behind me
Responding to prayers
Then a quiet lonely graveyard
Hidden from prying eyes.

*Anne, always a mum. A poem written by a mum
whose child died whilst she was in prison.**

Love and Pain

To write this I have opened a box
With you came a force of love of love
I'd heard it existed, like the mythical unicorn
But you brought it to me, it was within my reach
Our eyes met, the most beautiful being I'd ever seen
My heart enveloped you, it beats for you
I didn't see the evil coming for us
Locked away, traumatised, broken, apart from you
I longed to smell you, lay with you, breathe with you,
Seeing you then returning to my tin cage
How will I survive this, can I survive this
I wanted to grasp death, it felt like freedom
Love returned and conquered the black tormentor
Powered by your love, I couldn't leave
I couldn't let you believe mummy didn't love you enough
The flames of love burnt the black flames of death
The tin box, a torture room of pain, the home of the grim reaper
I will not allow it, he isn't taking my love,
Your love protects me
I survive for you, your true lionheart
This tormented separation, that neither of us chose
But I failed to protect us both
A wound on my heart, love and pain co existing
Love eclipses the pain, it thrives, and beats in ways pain can only dream of
You are the wonder of my world, mother son love
Cemented, ingrained in the sand scripts of time
To you I belong my boy.

Jennifer, a mum in prison.

Happy valetines DAY!

For Mummy

from your love, Eliza!

Eliza, aged ten.

CHAPTER 2

Poems Written by Children Who Have or Have Had a Parent in Prison

The poems in this section were authored by 'children' of all ages, our youngest poet was five-years-old, our oldest 'child' in his thirties—there is no cut-off point for being affected by parental imprisonment. Some of our older children are writing looking back over what they experienced as children, a couple are writing as adults, but also as the child of a parent imprisoned. Whatever their age, we see the impact having a parent in prison can have, and importantly how long that impact can last. Some are group poems, some are sole poems, some were written with the children, others posted to us by families, support workers, carers. Children's poems came to us from every corner of the UK, from Uganda, from Ireland, America and Canada. From whence they came the children shared experiences, good and bad—we saw common themes of bewilderment, anger, hurt, confusion and love.

Children need to be supported during this traumatic time, and families (often grandparents) who end up caring for them. Sometimes children have witnessed traumatic arrests, or were dropped off at school; neither they nor their parent having any idea how the day would end. Sometimes children are taken unexpectedly into care, either until family can be found to care for them, or with a view to foster care—sometimes leading to permanent adoption. Children and families need to be supported in communities and schools. As editors, we hope for a greater reduction in parents sentenced to custody, particularly primary carers, but are also hopeful that children of prisoners will be formally recognised, acknowledged and supported across a breadth of services, going at least some way towards reducing the harm caused to often invisible innocents.

We are grateful to all of our contributors for their bravery in allowing us to publish their words.

I Want My Mum

I want my mum
They took her-where
Where did they take her?
Prison they said
What does it look like, what does it sound like?
Will she be scared... I am scared?
I want my mum

Will she eat? Will I be able to see her? Phone her?
Will she miss my birthday? Will I get a present?
What will my friends say, I thought secrets were bad?
I want my mum

We have to stay here at nanny's—she smokes, it stinks
She cries, I cry, everyone cries
I don't care what she's done
I just want my mum.

Lucy, aged ten-and-a-half.

Dear Mummy

Dear Mummy
This poem is for you
I loved you from the day I was born
My brother loves you
But I love you more
I remember every single birthday
You me, me and you
I love you mum
I love our little crew.

Eliza, aged ten.

Eliza, aged ten.

Prison Time

I haven't seen my father
for 20 years
since he was sent to prison
I see men who look like him
On buses, on trains
In pub urinals

I visit prison
I hear clanking heavy metal doors
The echoing voices of men
Their morning breath and sallow skin
Who is the most free?
I walk through the metal
Deeper into the machine, the stern looks,
I feel guilt

The sins of the father handed down
I feel sorry for myself
So, your dad was in prison?
You can't decide what you have to digest
I was seven-years-old
Hardly anyone was like me

Now I'm back in prison
Time is nearly up
The guard knocks on the door
Out they file
Back to the belly of the prison
My students—in their armour.

Andy, aged 27.

Daddy Come Home

Daddy what are you doing
Why are you just sat there?
Why don't you just come home?
This table is silly
You look silly
You smell funny
You look funny
This is NOT funny
Daddy just come home.

Luke, aged nine.

Prison I Hate You

Prison you keep my mum from me
You stop her from being free
I need her home, I miss her so
Why can't you just let her go
I hate you prison, with all your bars
Id like to blow you up to mars
So, prison, tell me what I want to know
When oh when will you let my mum go?

Conrad, aged eight.

Eliza, aged eight.

Always

Mum's gone to prison
My world has come to an end
Wishing you were here
Helping with my fear
My love never goes mum
You made me who I am
I'm always going to love you
No matter where I am.

Zara, aged 14.

The Breeze

You left me young mum
I run down the stairs
To see your face every day
That makes me smile and glare
I stop and freeze
When I hit a breeze
I remember you're not there
But I know you always care

I love you Mummy.

Hakim, aged 12.

Stopping the Clocks

You can lock the locks, but you can't stop the clocks
The jail might be hell, but the people there really do care
You can stare at your four walls
But we are waiting for you in the hall
It won't be long before your free–on the other side of that wall
You may feel like you fallen–but we are going to hold you up
You may have had enough, but you'll be home soon enough
They can lock the locks
But stop the clocks…..
Daddy is home.

Emily, aged eight.

Be Good

Mummy you tell me to be good
To be kind, to be clever
I am, I'm a good girl
I don't want to go to prison
Not never
I want you to come home
So mum, say sorry
And mummy please be good.

Maria, aged eight.

I Miss My Daddy

I miss my daddy, even though he's bad
When I think of him, it makes me sad
I love my mummy
She looks after me
She gets my favourite things for tea
I don't like to go and see daddy
Because its far away
It makes me sleepy and I don't know what to say
THE END.

Alaiyah, aged five.

Dark

Imagine your worst nightmares bundled
into one feeling. That's the feeling
that people feel with a parent in prison.
Dark
Imagine having a Dad and then suddenly
he is gone. You can't touch him, feel him
its empty.
Dark.

Luke, aged eleven.

No Rules

Without him there were no rules
I didn't know anyone like me
With a dad in a prison
I felt alone and afraid
Different and weird
I wanted a friend and mate
Instead I got sneers, I got hate
I hated going to school
It seemed pointless to me
I didn't want to learn
My dad was in prison you see
I wanted to be like him
I thought he was cool
A rebel, a renegade
He followed no rules
I wanted to be like him
Now I'm in prison too
Be careful little children
This could be you.

Daniel, aged 24.

Goodbye

When I said goodbye
I thought I'd see you again
I thought you'd be home
It wouldn't be long
I thought it would go fast
You'd be home by Christmas
I told myself that
When I said goodbye
It wasn't forever
You're my dad
You belong with me
When I said goodbye, it wasn't forever
It wasn't for the last time
Why dad why
I was waiting
I was here
It wasn't meant to be forever
But you died in there
Soon became never.

Anonymous.

My Mum

My mum is very nice
She is pretty and she is kind
She likes to take me on adventures
But when we are tired of the adventures
We like to sit down on the benches
My mum is funny—she makes us laugh
She likes to make us bubble baths.

Leah, aged eight.

Polly, aged nine.

Alone

I don't know if I love him
He made my mummy very very very sad
He made me cry a lot
I was worried he would come back again
So, I didn't want to leave my mum
I couldn't do my work at school
I didn't want to go out
I was upset, I was worried
I was worried all the time
I didn't like to speak to my friends
Because they didn't know how I felt
I felt very very alone.

Millie, aged eleven.

Very

Dear dumb diary
He is called IT
He makes me feel very very very very very foreign
In my own world I feel foreign
Me and my sister feel very very very (x7) happy he's in prison
My sisters who are from IT are annoyed he did this
But they love him
We feel different to everyone else
I wish he was very very very very very very very
Very very very very very very very very very very
Very very very very sorry!
If I had a time machine
I would go back and put IT in a volcano
Where he would be never seen again.

Liam or Jacob, aged seven or 13 (depending on my mood).

Children of Prisoners

What kind of life is left to innocent children?
What image do you portray in the society?
Who is ready to pacify this situation?
And restore the lost love between parents and children
To quench and not quell the society
Where is the future for the prisoners' children?
What is their destiny and who is willing to predict?
All these traumatise children
And they became a pathetic figure
Because they are impelled by the situation

Children of prisoners
Nobody to extend love to them
But discrimination is always available
Who will embrace and not embroil these stars?
Because they are the next leaders
Who is coming up to speak for the rights of prisoners' children?
And bring justice in the country.

Rebecca, age unknown.

Untitled

Embarrassed
Humiliated
Punished
Abandoned
Ashamed
Frustrated
Isolated
Scared
Worried
Guilty
Lonely
Angry
Upset
Bad
Mad
Sad.

Luke, aged eleven.

Visiting Time

The bars, the dogs, the guards
They symbolse our time
Images of control of the state
They are between you and me
These symbols I hate

The hall is noisy, it reeks
Of pain, of sweat, of lost dreams
'No touching' they shout
Their eyes the drugs they seek

We are all criminals now
By association we are guilty
We can't be good, we can't be honest
We are related to criminals
So, logic tells them we are filthy

We are all touched by the shame
This place, it sucks us in
But who is to blame?
Is it you, is it me?
What led you to here?
It wasn't me
It was you
You and the Gear.

Joseph, aged 14.

Dear George

Dear George
I know you're my biological father
I know all that shit
I know you won't read this
Cause you're an idiotic prick
I know that sounds harsh
But really it's not
What's harsh is you left me
And I felt forgot
Imagine that feeling
All of your life
Imagine just dreaming
About how to die
How do you feel
Well I feel like shit
But you taught me one thing
Don't trust a prick
Cause of all of your promises
All of the lies

Look at me
I'm just like you dad
I'm turning into you
The lies
The people I've hurt too

So next time you think of robbing a house
Or selling drugs
I want you to remember
You can be someone else
You can start up our family
Give us a good life

I know it's a poem
But that's how I write

I'm giving you your final chance
Your final life
But this is not a game
You can't cheat but you can die
So, think before you act
Think of me and Ed
And little William
Think of us instead
Think of the fright
You think it is funny
You think it's alright
But it's not funny
And its not a good life

So, if these are our last words
Then I do love you dad
But I can't handle this
Your making me mad
I have anxiety
Depression and more
But the worst is
When I dry
Its cause I feel small
I don't have a father
But neither do a lot of kids
But I do understand
The hurt
The hatred
Because of one man.

Daniel, 'I made this all from scratch to show my father
how much I do miss him and love him'.

My Dad is in Prison

I feel like I am being punished too.
Sat waiting for the phone to ring.
Some people forget I have done nothing wrong.
I wish he could see me play football
No more cuddles or bedtime stories
Going to visits—highs and lows

Does he know I still love him?
Another birthday/Christmas without him
Doing time—counting down.

Luke, aged eleven.

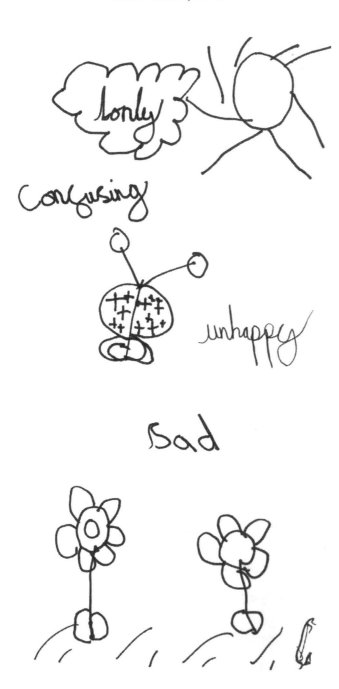

Charli-Mae was ten when she drew this.

Trinity's Rap

I was scrolling through Facebook
Saw a kid getting beat up — she only looked about eleven
How could you do that — kicked her in the face and about 20 in the back
Saw on the news that it was you
Can't believe that you would do that
Think about your daughter, how would she feel
When she found out you got sent down
For murder

She had a pretty rough time and music was her life
Went through a stage where she shut everyone out
Now she's coming out of her shell
Because her life had been hell
Now grown up with a family of her own
Forgetting about what you done to her dad when she was young

Met a new man, as the old one left
He wasn't good enough for her
Taking control of her past mistakes
Trying not to go through that stage again
Now she's got a dog
The icing on the cake

Things are looking-up, she got a promotion
Working with D J Khaled, songs going worldwide
Now she's scrolling through Facebook
No signs of kids being beat up
Her is now changed
She's a lot happier.

Trinity, aged 13.

Bring My Father to Me

Road to prison and road from prison
Bring my father to me
The sun is sinking and darkness is coming
Days are coming and days are going
But where is my father

My studies are stopped
My mother has also neglected me
I have nothing to eat and I have nothing to drink
I have only my grandmother and yet she is old
Return my father to me

Road to and from prison
I pray you return my father to me
A clear laughter in the village claiming I am a nobody
The son to a criminal, I neither have books nor pens
I have a torn blanket; I sleep on the mat in just a small hut
Where is my father
He could bring everything I needed
Road to and from prison
I implore you bring my father from prison

What should I do then?
All jobs need educated people
And some are given to their relatives
What should I do then?
I am lost on the mist
Please road to and from prison return my father to me.

Sharon, age unknown.

I Miss You

I miss your kisses, I miss your lips
I miss your rules and your cooking tips
The house isn't the same without you in it
The dog hates me, and Joel says 'innit'
The house is going to rack and ruin
The house isn't the same without you in
I'm rubbish at poems so I'll stop it now
I love you, we love you
We're taking a bow
The End.

Phoenix and Joel, aged ten and 14.

My Mum

What they said you did I don't believe
Not you not my mum
Why would you/
How could you
Not my mum
They took you away, they locked you up
In prison
In a prison
My mum
It can't be true
It can't be right
I watched the trial
I saw it all,
I heard it all
I can't think, I can't hear
I can't breathe
I can't believe
Not my mum
But you did
You admitted it
It was you
You're not my mum.

Poppy, aged 16.

When My Dad Went to Prison

My dad went to prison
I felt okay
Because I didn't like what my dad did
He did it to my mum.

Kayim.

It's Complicated

My Dad has failed and so has been jailed
And we are left behind
He was here one minute and gone the next
And nobody understands
It's like he has died but we have to hide
From what he has done

It's hard to describe how I still love my Dad
Even though he did something bad
Other people don't get it
And expect me to forget him
But love doesn't work like that
There is no on/off switch.

Sophie, aged 13.

Mummy of Mine

Mummy of Mine
I love you my mum
I miss you so much
I need to give you a kiss
I need to give you a cutch

I can't wait till your home
Back here with me
I'll be smiley and happy
I'll be good you'll see

We will read books and drink pop
We'll eat sweets till we drop
I love you my mummy, I'll never let go
Because mummy of mine I do love you so.

Meghan, aged ten.

Stars

Nothing is the same anymore
Nothing is predictable
I don't know where I am
I don't know where I'm going
I don't even know where I want to be
Except with them

I hate the visits, they smell
Its not me
It's not us
I guess it is now
I feel ashamed
I feel their shame
I wear their shame
It colours me

I don't know them
They don't know me now
How could they do this
How do I love them so much?
We share the same sky
The same stars

They look, I look
I can feel them
I miss them, I hate them
I hate stars.

James, aged 13, whose mum and dad were both in prison.

It Wasn't Us

My Dad did something wrong
And now I have to stay strong
He has years behind bars
I sit and stare at the stars
To take my mind off the pain
It hurts my body and brain

I wait for his telephone call
Hope its not when I'm playing football
It's so good to have a chat
About nothing much just this and that
To hear his voice and check he is fine
Even though its often a bad crackly line

At last we have a visit to see him for real
I am not really sure how I will feel
We have to travel a long way in the car
Prison visits are very often too far
It feels just like a roller-coaster ride
The highs of the visit and the lows of goodbye

Time inside goes very slow
Having to wait so long is such a blow
Whether you're the one inside or out
Counting down time, you want to scream and shout
But time on a visit seems to fly by
Soon they are shouting 'Say goodbye'.

Luke, aged eleven and Sophie, aged 13.

What You Don't See

There is something that many people don't see
There is something even parents don't see
Why do you commit crimes forgetting about us children?
You know what the law does
But what about us children?

There is something all of you don't see
There is something that even the government doesn't see
Consider us children of prisoners
Who serve the same punishment with our parents?
But what crime have I done?

Indeed, there is something many people don't see
There is something even the community doesn't see
Why do you punish me for my parent's crimes?
Like a refugee in my own community
Why do you put all the blame on me?

In case you don't know this
I will let you know it
There is something that many people don't see
There is something even the relatives don't see
I have no-one but you
To love and give me hope
To educate and support my future

But why do you also call me a curse
If you don't know, I will let you know
What kind of pain I suffer
I suffer insults, hatred, rejection, violence, injustice and defilement
I am forced to marry at such a tender age
And dying of HIV/AIDS
Please, consider my life because I also have a vision

Children of prisoners
Let's rise up together
And save our fellow ones
Who are still suffering injustice?
Because together we can make a difference.

Catherine, age unknown.

What About Me?

Lock him up, throw away the key they say
Three meals a day, TV in room, should be grateful they say
Visits and phone calls, don't deserve it they say
But what about me?

He is still my Dad whatever
His sentence is my sentence too
Punish him and punish me too

Do I not deserve to see my Dad?
A visit to see he is okay
A visit to talk about my day
A visit to have a hug.

Do I not deserve to speak to my Dad?
A call to say 'Hi'
A call to talk about my week
A call to say 'Good night sleep tight'.

What about me?

Luke, aged eleven.

My Baby Your Baby

I'm having a baby
I'm doing it alone, without you my mum,
My child will be walking before he knows you
I can't bring him there, I wont
He won't say grandma; how will he know you
How do I forgive you for this?
How do we make up the lost time?
Your baby is having a baby
And you are not here.

Miriam, aged 31.

You Don't See What I See

They do not see
How you would always wake me up
Before school
Cup of tea and toast in hand
But now I'm always late
And my teachers don't appreciate
That I'm now just a teen
With no routine
Because my Dad has gone
And I somehow have to push on

They do not see
How you were my mum and dad
Rolled into one
And now that you are gone
My 18-year-old sister
Has to be the one to wipe my tears away
When it gets to Christmas Day
And you aren't here
To listen to the music play
On Top of the Pops

They only see
What they want to see
A criminal
Written off from society
A Dad
Who left his children behind
In prison
Out of sight and out of mind
Just a man
Who could only be viewed as bad?
But that's not what I see
I just see my Dad.

Jodie, now in her twenties.

Daddy Love

My dad is tall
Although I fall
When he sits in a cell
It rings a bell
I caused it myself
It is damaging my mental health.

Aaron, aged eleven.

clay

friends.

days out.

nice food.

PIZZA.

nice clothes

Hannah, aged 13.

Good From Bad

My dad being in prison, personally changed me for the better.
Every event that's happened in my life has made me realise that it all
happened for a reason.
I wouldn't be where I am today.
I wouldn't have gone to Switzerland or been in a documentary.
As weird as it sounds, I sometimes thank my dad
For being as stupid as he is
Because him being stupid got me where I am today.
Him being stupid changed my view on life.
It proves all the good that comes out of the bad
Even if it is like having a piece of my heart missing.
I know I have friends and family to support me.
It can be like a mask with a fake smile.

Alex, aged 13.

What Happens When a Parent Goes to Prison?

You find out.
You get sad.
You go on visits.
They get day visits.
They get night visits.
They come home.
Remember, everything's okay!

Savannah, aged eight.

My Mate

Life with a dad is great
But now he's in prison
I've lost my mate
I trusted him to be there when I needed him most
But now I feel like I'm talking to a ghost
I'm angry, I'm hurt
I'm sad and I'm sacred
Because I didn't know I had to be prepared
I miss you dad and I love you lots
When you're free well go to the shops.

Jasmyn, aged eight.

We're Like Strangers

Three years ago, I was angry, confused and sad about my dad,
Knowing my dad got put away made me very mad.
If I was to see him today, I would be really shy, but why?
I know why, because we're like strangers.
Every time I see him, I get a little smile,
Knowing that we're family can make me a bit happy
And now I know what I want to be.

Peter, aged 12.

The Sound of Sirens

When I was four my mum and dad were sent to prison.
I remember the sound of sirens and lights flashing in.
Me and my brothers we were sent back to my nan's house.
My brothers were crying but I was too young to understand.
So, I got bought up by my nan and grandad.
My dad got released three years later when I was seven-years-old.
When he came out, I started to understand about the situation.
I felt like I was going to cry when he came out because I was so happy.
My other grandad died later on in my life.
I stayed off school because I was that sad.
My mum came out just before Christmas.
I was happy but I was scared because my mum and dad broke up.
So, I was hiding in my bedroom.
Every time my dad walked into the house, I would pretend to be fine
when I was actually upset.
I would play on my PS4 with my mates and look forward to school.
Because I was just too upset, I didn't feel like I could talk to anyone.
I wouldn't be where I am today if it wasn't for Lorna's groups.
They have helped me through this horrible journey.
Also, Red Ninja have helped me on my way and for that I am thankful.
I don't want other kids to go through what I have gone through.

Callum, aged eleven.

Seven-years-old

I was only seven-years-old when I was told my dad would be locked away
There was lots of talk, there still is today.
It's now four years later and my feelings are greater
I was disappointed but worried, it was all a bit hurried.
I go to see my dad on a visit but how far is it?
Used to be three hours but now it's only one hour
I think the guards have too much power
I was four minutes late and they shut the gate.
I was seven-years-old when I was told my dad would be locked away
But that has made me the person who I am today.

Macey, aged eleven.

Dear Mum

Why are you living in locked-up doors?
I never see you because your behind high brick walls
Why don't I see you every day?
There must be a reason you've gone away
Even though it's all broken I know I still have a home
But then again I'm all alone
I'm suffering with this built up facade
And people are beginning to feel alarmed
Tell me why someone else can't live this life
It kills me knowing you can't put me to bed every night
To this day I'm infatuated by my memories
The ones with you are so necessary
These moments are my walls
Which are bigger than them locked up doors
My experience is a question to be answered
Which I did these past nine years that I've counted
There is just one thing I weary
Never feel guilty for this unexpected journey
I have opportunities of a lifetime
What you did for me was far from a crime
It made me the person I am today
Even though you went away
I wouldn't change it in any way
We became one you and me
And forever your qualities will be the only thing I allow people to see
You want to know how I feel when you went away
The answer is, in so many different ways
I can't define what you've done for me
but one thing you will always be is my mummy.

Olivia, aged 17.

I Have a Memory

It's not comfortable to have a parent in prison.
That's what I think
I have a memory that my dad still lives with me.
But it is not like that.
Its uncomfortable to have a piece of your heart missing. But not forever.

Lauren, aged nine.

Horrible Sellings

It is uncomfortable to go through it.
But sometimes you do get through it.
I haven't yet.

Cerys, aged six.

Mummy's Castle

Mummy's in a castle
With big gates and barbed wires
Mummy's in a castle
With high fences and grand bushes
Mummy's in a castle
With plain furniture and ancient walls
Mummy's in a castle
With big dogs and concrete floors
Mummy's in a castle
With security guards and bolted doors
Mummy's in a castle
Where we only get to see her for two hours
Mummy's in a castle
Where she has to wear a bib
Mummy's in a castle
Where goodbyes are the hardest thing
Mummy's in a castle called prison.

Toni, now in her twenties, was six when her mum went to prison.[1]

---

1. See also Toni's mum's poem 'Looking Back' on page 47.

Snakes & Ladders

A parent in prison isn't that bad.
The child who has come to face this situation
Can sometimes go on visits.
Visits aren't all that bad either.
You can have Family Days.
Although you can have normal visits.
The parent in prison can start a game
Of Snakes and Ladders.
Your emotions go up the ladder.
And then when you find about the parent
The snake stops you.

Abbie, aged eleven.

Carry On With Your Life

Don't feel sad about the parent being away.
Carry on with your life and don't worry about the bad reasons.
People start to pick on you and call your dad mean things.
You get on with life, but you still think about the parent.
You tell your 'best' friend and they tell everyone.
You start to worry and think it's your fault.
You go on visits and see the parent, but you're still upset.
You're worried your parent hasn't stopped their bad actions.
Don't feel sad about the parent being away.
Carry on with your life and don't worry about the bad reasons.

Kyra, aged ten.

Echoes of Pain

Tears of blood running down my cheek
Clearly, I too bleed
About a pool of it because the feelings
o, o, o, so weak
In that pool I have done many things to disguise the pain for leaving you, I too
am weak
I can feel it in my veins coming out so slow
I feel you as I too have turned cold
It's a feeling of pain I wish I could let go
Pain I too wish to let go
It flows through my heart down to my toes
You are my heart the only truth I surely know
It's like a cart on a hill, it goes and goes
I spin as if I'm in a wheel, I too go and go
One day this shrill feeling will all burn away
I can only hope that burn will come quick as today
And a feeling of thrill will redeem it one day
It would be a thrill just to blow the ash away for you someday.

> *LaQuintae (age unknown) and her mother Tami.*
> *LaQuintae wrote lines of the poem and mailed it to her mom*
> *who is incarcerated. Tami then added to the poem in response,*
> *line by line and mailed it back to her daughter.*

Drawn by Luke when he was aged 12.

My Mum

My mum went away, and I was sad
I had to go live with my silly dad
I quite like him
But he's not my mum

My mummy is funny
She's kind and she's sunny
My dad thinks he is,
But he isn't funny

I missed my Mum
I wanted her home
I hated that she was in her bed on her own

I'm back with my mum
It feels good to me
Now I miss my dad
I wish we could be three.

Polly, aged nine years three months.

I Miss My Mum

I miss my mum
That's it
The End.

Annie, aged five.

Eliza, aged ten.

CHAPTER 3

Poems Written by Dads In and After Prison

In the UK alone 295,000 children are affected by paternal imprisonment, millions of children globally. Although we still don't know enough about the impact of this on children, we know a little more about he impact when it is a father who goes to prison than if it is a mother. However, what we know less about is how fathers manage their fathering emotions and their fathering role in and after prison. When we began collecting poems for this project, we were not sure that fathers would engage with us as well as mothers, but we couldn't have been more wrong. The fathers we met couldn't wait to speak about their children, whether they were in contact with them or not—they all had feelings and emotions they wanted to express about and for their children; whether around hope, or regret (or a mix of both) most were feelings related to love and loss. Some dads contacted us to say they had lost contact with their children but were keen to still feel like, and importantly be seen as, 'Dad'. Many saw their children as a source of hope and motivation as well as of love and pride. Several thanked us for including them, saying it was the first opportunity they had had to express their emotions in or after prison. This highlight the real importance of programmes such as 'Family Man' run by Safeground,[1] 'Invisible Walls' at HMP Parc,[2] 'Strength in Families' in Washington, USA, and 'Incarcerated Dads' in San Francisco.

We hope you will enjoy the powerful poems written by dads in and after prison, and we thank them for their contributions.

---

1. For more information and contacts please see www.safeground.org.uk/prisons/family-man/
2. For more information and contacts see www.g4s.com/media-centre/ our-views/all-news/invisible-walls-wales and also www.channel4.com/news/ dads-behind-bars-teaching-inmates-to-put-kids-before-crime-parc-prison-andy-davies

HOW ol feel

George, aged six, mum and dad in prison.

My Head Wasn't Right

My head wasn't right, I wasn't thinking
I wish I'd listened to your mum
When she said stop drinking
I committed my crime, it wasn't nice
Now sadly we ALL are paying the price
Christmas is coming, I should be at home
But instead I'm sat here and I'm all alone

I know its Christmas and you'll have your fun
Don't worry kids
I'll be home for the next one.

Jay, a dad in prison.

When Did I Last See Sky?

When did I last see sky?
It was so long ago
I can't see flowers
I can't see trees
I can't smell baking
I can't think
I can't find peace
This place it eats me up
Swallows me whole
It takes my liberty
It takes my soul
I want to be free
I want to be me
I want to see the sky
I want to feel the breeze
My children where are you?
Don't forget me
Time will pass
Time, hurry please.

Dave, a dad in prison.

Generations of Crime

My grandad was here
My dad was here
Now I'm here
Was this always my fate?
A place of pain, of violence
A place full of hate
It kept me from you
From grandad too
All I wanted was to play
To see you, kiss you too
To come home and stay
Now I'm here
But I have to get out
This isn't for me
I'm not that one
I have to stay out
I need to be with you
To bet there for my son.

Seamus, a dad in prison, son and grandson of ex-prisoners.

And I Need My Dad

You are not here
Like my friend's dad
To build rocket-ships
And kick a football.
You are not here
To give me a hug
And put me to bed
Like you used to.
You are not here
To walk me to school
And cheer for me
On Sports Day.
You are not here
To dry my tears
And make me safe
When I am afraid.
You are not here
When mum needs a hug
Or when she needs
A shoulder to cry on.
You are not here
Because you are there:
Inside doing time,
And I need my dad.

Mark, post-prison dad of two boys.

The Impetus for Positive Change

She battled her own conscience
Brought you through those doors
The brutal noise of clanging gates
Of guards' boots upon the floor

They wouldn't let me touch you
Or smell your new born skin
Reinforced glass stopped us
I took it on the chin

I wouldn't let me show you
Just how bad I felt inside
As I struggled with those demons
My smile was big and wide

Yet you, you were oblivious
To all those adult worlds
To how you changed my life
So, our story could unfold

As though our start had been stalled
A transformation had begun
I could do no other
Than be a real father to my son

And now your twenty-five
A success in your own right
You told me once I'd inspired you
By fighting the good fight.

David, an ex-prisoner, now proud dad and social worker.

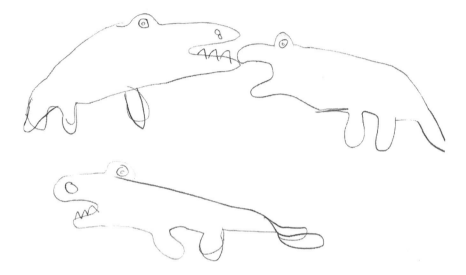

Jimmy Lee, aged nine.

My Sons

I'm proud of being a dad
To my lovely sons
It's magical, it's inspiring
We have so much fun
They are always here to make me smile
Exciting, having fun
It's enjoyable being a dad
My sons are priceless to me
I will always love them
For eternity
Even from in here.

Simon, a dad in prison.

My Best Friend

I tell anyone who'll listen, 'I had him for more days than his mum actually'
He shouted at the waves like a Viking
'I don't need anybody's help, I do it by myself'
He bounced into the sea and froth, fearless three-year-old
Played with until the sun dipped below the Suffolk horizon
His lips and toes were blue
I chased him, up and down, a dozen trains
And still now I wonder
How the inside of a stuffy carriage is more fun
Than staring out of a window
At trees, birds, back gardens, calm canals and sky

I'm not convinced of a more powerful sleeping pill
Than the tired cuddle of a child
We waved at planes, taking off and landing,
Marched with unwashed anti-frackers,
Cheered the rain, poked sticks in camp fires
Swam in rivers and ate carrot cake for breakfast
He pushed along on his hand me down scooter
Until the pavement turned to grass

I sang him the songs, banned by vegan parents
Fighting guilty pangs when his eyes danced
He mouthed along to 'Old MacDonald had a farm'
Where did he learn them?
Up and down the country we went
Seeking parks, slides swings and duck ponds
Always singing
E-i E-I Oh.

Liam, a prison dad.

Don't Worry—A Fairy Tale

Once upon a time there was a beautiful little face
Who without any effort deserved her name of Grace
Now every night she liked to hear stories
Of princesses, castles and boats on high seas
In a bedroom of pink, they would lay and read
Imagining a prince about to be freed
Until one day when it all stopped
Her father, the king of the world disappeared
So, each night she dreamed her happy ending
And day after day she found herself waiting
Then one night her father's voice came as she slept
And in the morning when she remembered, she wept
Don't worry her father said, I'm okay
I'll hope and I'll pray and I'll blow love your way

Under the light of a distant star
A child was born free
He was a magical sight, this boy named Amani
A strong little character he would grow to be
Determined and knowing what he needed to see
Loving and loved he knows what he wants
Which every night were his dad's big hugs
Until one day when it all stopped
And his dad the strongest man in the world had gone away
Thereafter each night his nightmares came true
As day after day he waited for dad to come through
Then one night his dad's voice came as he slept
An in the morning he remembered and he gently wept
Don't worry dad said I'm okay
Ill hope and pray and blow love your way

Before this fairy tale is done there's another one
A beacon of light by the name of Brian
Now he loved his daddy so very much he wouldn't share
He couldn't be alone, he wanted to go everywhere
On the kitchen counter he would sit and look
Taking tips from daddy and watching him cook
Until one day when it all stopped and
His daddy the best in the world went missing
So each night he asked his mum where daddy had went
Day after day he waited for news to be sent
Then one night, his daddy's voice came to him as he slept
In the morning he remembered and he gently wept
Don't worry daddy had said, I'm okay
Ill hope and ill pray and ill blow love your way

The next day the children sat together to play
Where they remembered the word, their daddy would say
Don't worry daddy the children said, Were okay
We love you and miss you and blow love your way
Together we pray we'll see you again one day.

Simon, a dad in prison.

My Son

My son my son
What example am I
Teaching you to steal and lie
I need to be a better man
I'm here I'll try
I'm doing all that I can

I want to be home, be there for you
Your mum, your sister and the new baby too
My son my son
Please don't be like me
Be good be honest
Then you'll stay free.

Will, a dad in prison.

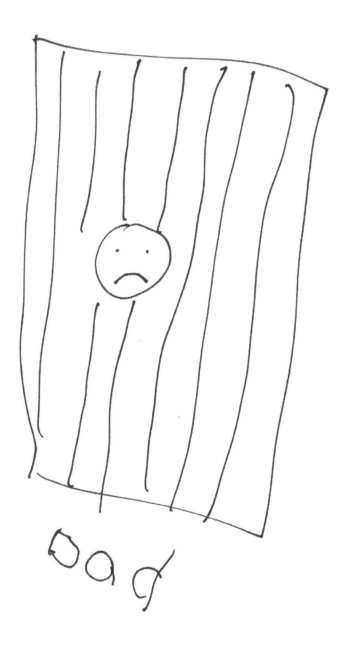

Thomas, aged seven.

Wings

I wish I had wings
So I could fly away
To leave my stress and worries
For just one day

To have wings like a bird
And fly up to the sky
And leave this life I chose as a boy

Because freedom is what I want
Freedom is what I need
Even though I don't have wings
I still believe
That free I will be
And free I will stay
Never to lead this life gain
To be dad instead.

Daz, a dad in prison.

Waves

I let the waves in my mind crash over me, washing my head
  Cleaning my thoughts of crime and time still to spend
 I feel like I'm drowning, I can't find the surface
I can't swim to the top
  I need a life jacket, I need life to find me, to hold me
    Not rescue, not that, I need to save myself
  In doing so, in freeing myself from the waves
I will then save you from drowning, from stepping in the water
    At all
I must free myself from the water
    For my children.

Abdul, a dad in prison.

Love

I'm supposed to be there
I'm supposed to be out
I'm supposed to love you
I'm supposed to shout
At the monsters that scare you
I'm supposed to love you
How can I from here
I'm supposed to be there
I'm not supposed to be here.

Frank, a dad in prison.

Princess

Your birth can be described as magical
I looked at you with thoughts of admiration
It was the proudest day of my life
Bursting with excitement I hugged you
A priceless moment
I saw you smile and realised I've never felt a love like this
Watching you grow, inspires me to do better
Quality time, having fun, so enjoyable
Although I'm away for now await the day
To return to you after a time so fraught
I want you to know not for a second did you leave my thoughts.

Ranx, a dad in prison.

My Little Dinosaurs

Got a twelve-year sentence, will do six
My life's one big mess, I'm falling to bits
Missing my two little boys, can't get a decent night's rest
Every day a struggle, can't cope with the stress

Two little boys lost without their dad
Two little boys all upset and sad
Don't know whether they are coming or going
Or who to tun to when they cry
Wondering
Why did daddy leave me?
And why he never said goodbye

I wish I could tell you my little dinosaurs
I wish I could pick up the phone to ring you
I wish I could write you a letter
But more, I wish I was beside you

Its as hard for me as it's hard for you
I wish you could understand
But daddy's not left you
Because he doesn't love you
He's just been a silly billy man

He just has to be away for a bit
To get help for the mistakes he's done wrong
To make a better future, to stop him doing wrong again
So don't see this as a punishment
Instead a second chance

For daddy to be a better man
For daddy to be a winner
For daddy to be a decent man
To sit with you and eat our dinners

So even if I'm not around
You've got mummy by your side
Don't be afraid to talk to her
Or afraid to break down and cry

You're only human daddy's boys
Trust me I tell no lies
There's not a day goes by
That daddy don't break down and cry

So don't let no-one tell you different
Or even call you weak
Cos no matter how big and hard you are
It takes a bigger man to weep

Don't get me wrong there's been times
When I've wanted to be with your sister
In the heavenly skies above
But what sort of father would I be
To leave you for ever and ever
Without a kiss, a goodbye hug

But leaving you with the questions
Was it me and why?
What sort of father would that make me?
What sort of father am I?

Miss you my little dinosaurs.

Martin, a dad in prison.

Jailbreak by Finnlay, aged eleven.

My Children You Suffer

My children you suffer
What have I done?
What did I do?
What have become
It's right that I'm here
To atone for my crimes
I was out of control
Stealing time after time

I pretended there were no victims
I stole from the rich not the poor
But of course, that's not true
The real victims are you

Daddy is sorry, he is ashamed too
He will be a better man
Because of his love for you
I'll make it up to you soon
When I get out of this place
The old dad he's gone
Of him there's no trace

My children you suffered
For all of my crimes
I've broken my promises time after time
I'm coming home soon and then we will be
Happy, united, together we three.

Marshall, a dad in prison.

Me and daddy when he gets out. Bobby, aged seven.

Blessin Jasper Lee in 2011

I was presented with a beautiful blessin
This blessin was my son Jasper Lee
I first got to meet him at the age of three
He taught me to be strong,
Forgiving, loyal truthful and strong
Those are some of life's lessons that cannot be left as a thought
But are continuously practised and taught
Because they can easily be forgotten
I can't ever say I forgot because
Every time I see my son
He doesn't let me forget
It's like listening to the No 1 hit
Every time you turn the radio on
Ask me for my teacher
And ill give you my eleven-year-old son
He has helped me realise that I have already won
My job as a father is never done.

Situf, a dad in prison.

138

Wells of Hope

You reached out to our broken hearts and mended our family's shaken relationships
When injustices befell us, when the gruesomeness of my crime distressed us
When my heart got empty, and my hands were empty
In my empty hands you put the gift of hope
When I had none, you brought back the moment of contentment
I lost it all

I drink of the cup of solitude and loneliness
I begot the chalice of void and hurt,
I was saddened by pain, the wrath of my bad deeds
Followed me with my distress
I got hungry and my stomach emptied.
I got thirst that no water would quench.
I became a victim of injustice
Even the innocent children of mine were affected
I saw tremors of horror and terror in my family

But…
Before I lost it all, I found you
Oh no! you found me
You built a bridge between me and my family.
You gave me knowledge and skills to give to my children
Amidst lack and derivation
You reached out to my family
At the time only darkness filled their ways
You brought trust back to us when joy and dreams seemed dead
You reached my daughter when my hand was shortened
It is still dark, and darkness still surrounds me
But I am not afraid, for the movement of good works
Flowed by love
You give us HOPE.

Pascal.

A Second Chance

A second chance at happiness
A second chance at love
To be a husband and a father again
I implored the lord above

He answered my prayer
In all its Glory
Now I provide guidance,
Help with homework
And read bedtime stories

To be home with them
To make sure they're safe
That is my greatest desire
So I'll take those parenting classes
Seek out advice
I'd even walk through fire
Sometimes I can't believe this blessing I've received
Two more daughters, two more sons

Sometimes I can't believe this blessing I've received
A second chance at happiness
A second chance at love.

James, a dad in prison.

CHAPTER 4

Group Poems

Group poetry is a wonderful way for participants to engage this type of writing, especially those who are less confident writers. The group poems were collected from a number of resources which included prisons, prison mother and baby units, residential alternative to custody services, and services supporting children with imprisoned parents. One poem was even collected on a coach taking children of imprisoned parents to an away day treat! The poems were collected either directly by the editors or by facilitators already working with groups or individuals in groups for which we are most grateful.

The group poem process for this book used a technique which involved the participants agreeing headings and titles for their poems and the poem verses — the group members then would each write a line related to that heading. Their lines were then collated and developed into a poem and read back to the group to agree — no words that were not in the members' lines were ever added. Without exception the groups loved their created poems and were always moved and proud of what they had achieved, using their voices to express their emotions and describe their feelings. As one group member wonderfully phrased it, *'Together we are louder, we are harder to ignore'*.

Rainbows and Unicorns

My mind is carefree and fun,
Filled with rainbows and unicorns,
And wonderful things,
No worrying, just playing and dreaming,
Of what life will bring,
What could change this,
And make it so bad?
Well, I'll tell you,
The imprisonment of my mum and dad.

Suddenly with no warning,
The roles have changed,
I'm worrying about my parents,
As my visit is arranged,
I'm lonely, I'm frustrated,
It's such a long way to go,
For such a short two hours,
It makes me feel so low,
I'm confused because they,
Did something bad,
But I don't want to leave them,
It makes me so sad.

A wrench on the heart,
Every visiting time,
I'm worried are they coping,
As they stand back in line,
Buses, trains, taxis, so long,
Exhausting, embarrassing,
How did this go so wrong?

How do they manage?
What will others say?
Who do you trust with this stuff?
Who will think it's okay?
School is a trial,
But I'm slowly getting through
I hope my parents learn
From the things that they do.

*Written collectively, by 40 children, being supported by
the charity Children Heard and Seen, during a bus trip to
the London Eye funded by charitable donations.*

Georgia, now in her twenties, who has experienced both parents in prison.

Family Ties (1)

Before

I was lost, I was scared
Dependant on alcohol.
I was angry, I was scared to breathe.
All I wanted was a family.
I felt my bump growing
As it got bigger—so did my worry.

In prison

I feel alone, I'm on my own,
I feel like I can't do this
But I can, I can
Everyone watches me
But prison has saved me
My baby came!
I finally know true happiness
I'm no longer lost
I am found.

Looking forwards

I *will* show everyone
I can do this
Ill be a brilliant mum
A family, with dad too maybe
Well go on holidays
Ill spoil them
Ill be a proud mum
I AM a proud mum.

*Written by Courtney, Sarah and Melissa—all mums resident with
their babies in a prison Mother and Baby Unit in the North.*

Warrior Queen

Slow motion pain for four years
Internal bleeding no-one sees
Suspended in time, my heart getting colder every day
Tortured in tears
Agonising in solitude
Nowhere to smile
No Mum
Left to suffer in loneliness
Our home empty
No perfume in the house
No hugs
No Warrior Queen who would kill for us
Left to suffer in silence and to blame her.

Written by the five children of Paula, a mum who went to prison.

Me and my friends by Jimmy Lee, aged nine.

Family Ties (2)

Before

I was irresponsible, a poorly man,
But, loving and caring dad always
I put my family first,
Loving, always showing I cared
I worked all day, we ate together
We had fun, on my bike, at the park,
in the grass, walks by the river
We laughed, we cuddled,
Waking up — hearing your laughter
Exciting new adventures,
I wanted you to have the life I never had
Settling you to sleep
I was always there
I just loved you.

Being a dad in prison

I'm lonely, I'm lost, too much time to think
It's horrible here, I miss you
I miss being able to protect you, miss playing silly games
Miss buying you everything
Just miss you
I can't be a dad here, its crap
I see you excited on visits, we share drinks on visits
—then sad to leave, I watch you go
I feel helpless, disappointed I'm not there
Every day I think of you
What are you up, how can I be a better dad?
I've let you down,

I'm missing you growing up
I need to be strong, be your role model
I look at your pictures, I miss you more
I love you more than anything
It's hard — being a dad in prison.

Looking forwards towards release

I want to plan, spend time with you, breather
I want to holiday with you, take you shopping,
Teach you things
I want to be a dad again, to provide to watch you grow
I can't wait to be together, to watch TV, to snuggle on the sofa
To be back how we were, I'll be proud
I'll watch you smile, watch you laugh
I want to have Christmas together, I can't wait for that
To be at home, just be a dad, a grandad
I want us to be cooking and laughing, dancing!
You are my princess
You are here with me — behind the keys and the locks
You make me strong, you are my life
My family will be back together — the way it should be
Please give me a chance — to have our relationship again
I want to spend time with you
I will show you
Give you all my lost love,
Do everything together
Even travel the world fare and wide
I will rise again
I will be there.

I'm out now — imagine that

I'm making up for lost time, I'm free
Finally, we laugh, we play, we are silly
You are here with me,
Spending time in my space,
I'm spending time in your space
This smile will never frown
I'm working hard, I will provide
We are reunited
I'm so happy we are together again
The way it should be
I'm not going again
Believe me
Every birthday with you
Watching the starts whilst you fall asleep
It's me putting you to bed, each night
I'll be there when you wake
More chapters of your life to come
I'm here, all the way
I'm not going back
You make me smile, you make me laugh
I promise
It won't be like before
I'm back watching your success
Back with my sons, back with my princess
Playing in the sand, ice cream and sweets
I'm on top of the world, I'm working so hard
I'll make you laugh I'll make you proud
I'm sorry for the past
I love you all
My family
I'm sorry.

*Dads in a northern English prison, including a father
and son: Rudy, Darren, John, Ashley, Ross, Jake, Luke,
Gareth, Davinder, Malcolm, Simon and Ranjit.*

Time

Before...
I was strong, a rock, positive
Wild nasty, I was a victim
I was fake
I loved a chase
A loving mum still, us against the world
Caring confident, over protective ...fun
Stubborn, I expected more
I was not fun as a mum

In prison...
I'm broken, I'm helpless, I have no control
I'm sad
Desperately trying to be part of their lives
There's pain, there's worry
I feel lost, I feel I've lost my heart,
I feel I've failed, I feel alone
I'm broken, I'm fighting, I realise my family is important
I'm working hard, I'm improving
I'm wiser, I'm forgiving
I'll think twice

Looking forwards to release.......
I'm excited, I'm happy, looking forward
I understand them now, they need fun
They need me
I'm anxious, uncertain, I'm fearful
I'm scared—it will be alright though
Wont it?
Ill get to know them, I'll be fun
I will be mum embarrassing, supportive and funny
I'll listen, I'll play, ill cuddle
I'll make new memories
I'll have you in my life
I'll make good plans

I'm out......
I'm looking after my family, I'm free
I don't take you my children for granted
I'm proud, my words now actions
We have time, holidays, memories
We love, we care, we have fun we laugh
We love
Precious time
Making up for lost time
It's not the same
But I'm hoping it will be
Only time will tell......

*Group poem written by the Mothers Inside Out Group
in a women's prison in 2018: Adel, Danielle, Sam,
Diane, Pham, Rosie, Natacha, Vera and Alexandra.*

Me and My Addiction

I had all the time in the world for my children
I was a good mum, I loved them with all my heart
I was content and confident that you were my world
But sadly my addiction took over and we had to part
First time mum, I didn't know where this was going
I'd never been clean before
We would always be laughing and having fun
I was confident happy and glowing
Nothing would get in the way
I wasn't a parent before my addiction, I didn't know what to expect
The love I have for you was untold
Before too long my addiction would unfold

It started off fine, just once a week wasn't that bad
Although I still love you and cared for you
I was selfish and put my needs first
My addiction took over and my actions were slack
It's now a distant memory, I don't like to look back
I was caring, but not enough to stop
Although I was addicted, I still loved you, you were still my baby
I was sad, depressed and so deeply lost
All my feelings were sticking to him like a magnet
I could only imagine I wouldn't be a good parent
Then most days I found it hard to cope, it made us all sad
My addiction got in the way
I felt so disconnected
The power of addiction and making bad choices
My own selfish needs, not realising you're all I need
All the bad memories of using crack are still in my head
Because of that drug me and my other kids are apart
All I wanted was alcohol to numb my soul
Wanting to forget all the bad things that happened
It was all about me

Has left me with heartache and hearing those voices
The warm sensation of the drink going down my throat, making the troubles
disappear
My thoughts and feelings began to take control

Addiction almost took my child away from me
Once day my sweet baby I will forever hold you
I'm free of addiction and a step closer to you
Yes, now I'm drug free at last
I will no longer have to hide under a mask
You'll always be my number one
He will have a mummy that is all there with love and care
I'm not carrying all the weight on my shoulders, no more, I am free
I'll always be there for you, anytime you need me
My confidence will return but there is so much I have to learn
I can be there when you need me
Our future will be in our hands

I was seven years clean before — our life was fab
Our life is getting better day by day
The day has come you're forever mine
We spend a lot more time as a family, laughing and playing away
My life is better, brighter
I don't lie to myself or you anymore
Full of new experience and laugher
I know I can do it now, I'm ready in my heart I'm glad
I'm happy with myself now
My children are happy and so am I, now I can spread my wings and fly
This is me and how I want my life to be
Together we will forever shine.

This and the following poem are both from Trevi House.

Me as a Mum

I thought I would be that perfect parent
The one from the book that doesn't exist
Loving, doting and trusted
I thought I would be the best parent
Determined to always be there no matter what
I thought I'd be patient, always put you first
Always be there for you, when you needed me the most
That there would be no rules
You would get away with everything
There's no such thing as perfection
Love, care and safety is a short selection
I thought I would be a great mum
The most caring and loving one
All I wanted was a baby to love and to love me
I didn't get much love as a child
So all my lost love I can give to thee

I am kind, calm, patient and funny
I love my child unconditionally
As a mummy to you I give you my all
My love for you will never stall
I'm always there to listen, even when it's hard
I could be more patient, but I couldn't be more proud
Sometimes I was unintentionally distant and low
They had their physical needs met,
but nowhere for their feelings to go
I'm a good, loving, caring parent
I spoil you to the max
I may sometimes be wrong
For giving you gifts you don't really need
I'm a great mum, I love you so much indeed

Now I am back, better than I was before
It's all about my children now, and forever more
I want to be a mum that doesn't shout or scream
One that has lots of love, always kind never mean
I want to be always there for you, no matter what
The one you can feel safe and secure with
Bring the best out of you, let you be what you want to be
Do everything in my power to keep you safe and happy
I want to be only the best for you
And that's exactly what I will do
The best parent for my precious baby,
The parent that everybody wants to be
The perfect parent.

Group poems by Anna, Charlie, Fi, Jolene, Karen and Mariya, all residents of Trevi House (an alternative to custody residential resource for mums recovering from addiction—residents have sometimes been to prison in the past and were at risk of a custodial sentence when referred to Trevi).

The Two of Us

Having a father in prison isn't as bad as they all think
I met my dad when I was 10 years old,
ever since then we've been the best of friends
sometimes it gets hard—I can't call him hang out etc
But I always remember he'll be home soon
Having a father like mine is like watering a plant
I am the seed of the plant, once he started to water this plant, I started to grow
I was once intimidated by his intelligence but as time has passed, I have slowly become
this guy.

Being a father in prison isn't as bad as you think it is
Actually, it can save your life
Before that first loving embrace, there were inspirational, uplifting and impressive
conversations held with a 10-year-old
The realization that this beam of beautiful light was someone that I helped create
Was the hope I needed to conquer any obstacles.
Pain was a frequent visitor, as I felt my physical presence should have been there
To cheer her accomplishments
But there is blessing in the connection. Though I gave her the flame
To let her blaze, there were many times I had to look at her to keep my fire lit.
Raising a daughter from prison isn't always as bad as it seems.

There is nothing more I wish for him than peace, joy and prosperity when he's home.
I've learned there's a reason for everything and a positive for every negative.
A day will come when we will talk, laugh, hug, etc without a time limit,
When we will take trips, spend good time, for holidays and more.
I miss him every day hes in there, but I appreciate him
The whole time he was my father, he raised me
From whatever position he was in, and is still raising me now
I love him and no matter what tries to stand between us
That could never expire.

The beauty of life has bloomed before my eyes, and knowledge
That there is an eternal love shines within, allowing me to walk with an aura
The success that is to come with my physical liberation will first come in the time
and energy spent with family.
Moments are sacred, a lesson learned, whilst conducting life 20 minutes at a time
or creating quality time
Within community centre environment
I walk without fear, full of courage and hope.
I remain humble in my duties, I can be called many things
But 'father' is definitely one of my favourites.

Poem written by a dad in prison and his daughter on the outside,
daughter's words in italics: Jon, and his daughter Jzahlisi.

Some Useful Resources for Families Affected by Imprisonment

Children Heard and Seen (CHAS)
Charity supporting children and families with a parent in prison.
childrenheardandseen.co.uk

Partners of Prisoners Support (POPS)
Charity supporting families of prisoners that works to influence positive developments.
www.partnersofprisoners.co.uk

Families & Friends of Prisoners
Voluntary organization based in Wales providing support and advice.
ffops.org.uk

Families Outside
Scottish charity working solely to support families affected by imprisonment.
Helpline 0800 254 0088
www.familiesoutside.org.uk

Action for Families Enduring Criminal Trauma (AFFECT)
Supports families and friends of those serving or facing prison sentences.
affect.org.uk

St Nicholas Trust
Supports families of prisoners in Ireland.
www.stnicholastrust.ie

Prison Advice and Care Trust (PACT)
Charity that provides support to prisoners, people with convictions and families, including to make a fresh start.
Helpline 0808 808 2003
www.prisonadvice.org.uk

Prison Reform Trust
Independent national charity operating an advice and information service for friends and families of prisoners.
www.prisonreformtrust.org.uk

St Giles Trust
Charity helping people facing severe disadvantage to find jobs, homes and lead positive lives.
www.stgilestrust.org.uk

My Time
Community support of children aged five to 18 years who have a parent in prison.
www.mytimeltd.org.uk

International Coalition for Children of Imprisoned Parents
Strives to strengthen global relationships of devoted organizations, institutions, individuals and students by uniting their 'many scattered voices'.
inccip.org/about-us-3

Two further Waterside publications using poetry as an antidote to crime and punishment

www.WatersidePress.co.uk